I0448411

February 2013

DEPOT MAINTENANCE

Additional Information Needed to Meet DOD's Core Capability Reporting Requirements

GAO

Accountability ★ Integrity ★ Reliability

Highlights

Highlights of GAO-13-194, a report to congressional committees

DEPOT MAINTENANCE

Additional Information Needed to Meet DOD's Core Capability Reporting Requirements

Why GAO Did This Study

DOD uses both military depots and contractors to maintain many complex weapon systems and equipment. Recognizing the key role of the depots and the risk of overreliance on contractors, Section 2464 of Title 10 of the U.S. Code requires DOD to maintain a core maintenance capability—a combination of personnel, facilities, equipment, processes, and technology (expressed in direct labor hours) that is government-owned and government-operated—needed to meet contingency and emergency requirements. Section 2464 directs DOD to provide a Biennial Core Report to Congress and include three elements: (1) core capability requirements, (2) planned workloads, and (3) explanations and mitigation plans for any shortfalls between core capability requirements and planned workloads. In response to a requirement in Section 2464, GAO assessed the extent to which the report complied with the statute and included supporting information from the services as required by DOD. GAO reviewed relevant legislation, DOD's 2012 Biennial Core Report, the services' submissions to support the report, and related DOD guidance.

What GAO Recommends

GAO recommends that DOD improve its Biennial Core Report by including detailed explanations of why the services do not have the workload to meet core maintenance requirements for each identified shortfall. In written comments on a draft of the report, DOD concurred with the recommendation.

View GAO-13-194 For more information, contact Zina D. Merritt at (202) 512-5257 or merrittz@gao.gov.

What GAO Found

The Department of Defense's (DOD) 2012 Biennial Core Report complies with two of the three biennial reporting elements of Section 2464 by including information on core capability requirements and planned workloads available for maintaining these requirements. The Office of the Secretary of Defense (OSD) reported core capability requirements totaling about 70 million direct labor hours for the military services. Also, OSD reported a total of about 92 million direct labor hours for planned workloads with an estimated cost of about $12 billion. OSD reported complete information on core requirements and planned workload at the top-level categories, such as Sea Ships, of the work breakdown structure. The statute directs that this information be organized by work breakdown structure, which is a group of categories of equipment and technologies. The top-level category—an entire type of system or equipment—can be broken down into lower levels of detail or subcategories, such as Aircraft Carriers or Submarines, that make up the system or equipment. DOD's overall planned workloads exceed its core capability requirements, but the report shows shortfalls in certain categories for the Army and the Air Force.

The report partially complies with the third biennial reporting element. DOD's report includes information on shortfalls at the top-level categories and plans to mitigate all shortfalls—where requirements exceed planned workload—identified in the report. However, the report does not include required information on the rationale for some of these shortfalls—reasons why the services do not have the workload to meet core requirements. The Navy and Marine Corps did not identify any shortfalls and were not required to provide explanations or mitigation plans. The report includes mitigation plans for shortfalls identified by the Army and the Air Force but does not always provide detailed explanations for why the Army and Air Force do not have sufficient planned workload to meet core requirements. The report does not always include detailed explanations for identified workload shortfalls, because the Army and Air Force did not always provide explanations for them. Without reporting clear explanations for why the services have shortfalls, Congress does not have visibility on whether the services' plans to correct or mitigate the shortfalls will address the cause of the shortfalls.

Extent to Which the Report Complies with the Required Biennial Reporting Elements in Section 2464

Required elements	GAO assessment
The core depot-level maintenance and repair capability requirements and sustaining workloads, organized by work breakdown structure expressed in direct labor hours.	Complied
The corresponding workloads necessary to sustain core depot-level maintenance and repair capability requirements, expressed in direct labor hours and cost.	Complied
In any case where core depot-level maintenance and repair capability requirements exceed or are expected to exceed sustaining workloads, a detailed rationale for the shortfall and a plan either to correct, or mitigate, the effects of the shortfall.	Partially complied

Source: GAO analysis of DOD data.

Note: Data are from DOD's Biennial Core Report.

Contents

List of Abbreviations

DOD   Department of Defense
OSD   Office of the Secretary of Defense

United States Government Accountability Office
Washington, DC 20548

February 11, 2013

Congressional Committees

The Department of Defense (DOD) maintains many complex weapon systems—such as aircraft and ships—and equipment—such as generators and radars—that require regular and emergency maintenance to continue being available for DOD to meet national security goals. To sustain these systems and equipment, at the depot level,[1] the department uses a combination of military depots—public-sector facilities that are government-owned and government-operated—and private-sector contractors. Depots play a key role in sustaining the complex weapon systems and equipment both in peacetime and during surge conditions like those created by the ongoing conflict in Afghanistan. Through these depots, DOD has what is referred to as the "capability" to perform needed repair work by maintaining a combination of skilled personnel, facilities, equipment, processes, and technology for each category of maintenance work being done.

Recognizing the important role of the depots in supporting U.S. forces and the risk of overreliance on private contractors for vital military needs, Congress enacted legislation in 1984 that exempts certain core maintenance activities identified by the Secretary of Defense from being contracted out.[2] The statute was later codified at Section 2464 of Title 10 of the United States Code and has been amended several times. Among other things, Section 2464 requires DOD to

- maintain a "core depot-level maintenance and repair capability"—a maintenance and repair capability that is government-owned and operated to provide a ready and controlled source of technical

---

[1]Depot maintenance is an action performed on materiel or software in the conduct of inspection, repair, overhaul, or the modification or rebuild of end-items, assemblies, subassemblies, and parts, that, among other things, requires extensive industrial facilities, specialized tools and equipment, or uniquely experienced and trained personnel that are not available in lower-echelon-level maintenance activities. Depot maintenance is a function and, as such, is independent of any location or funding source and may be performed in the public or private sectors.

[2]Pub. L. No. 98-525 § 307 (1984). This section was originally codified at 10 U.S.C. § 2304 (note).

GAO-13-194 Biennial Core Report

competence and resources to ensure effective and timely response to mobilizations, contingencies, or other emergencies and

- assign these government-owned and operated facilities (the depots) sufficient workload[3] to ensure that the department can maintain cost efficiency and technical competence during peacetime while preserving the ability to respond to a mobilization, contingency, or emergency.

DOD has a process to implement this statutory requirement in which the services are required to use a computational methodology to identify their essential core capability requirements and the planned workloads[4] to help support this core maintenance capability. The services are then required to submit biennially to the Secretary of Defense an internal report that summarizes the results of this process and identified shortfalls between requirements and planned workload.

In 2009, we reported that DOD, through this internal biennial reporting process, had not comprehensively and accurately assessed whether it had the required core maintenance capability to support systems currently in use in the military depots.[5] We found, among other things, that DOD's method of compiling and internally reporting core capability requirements and planned workloads did not reveal shortfalls between the requirements and the planned workloads for specific categories of weapon systems or equipment that we had identified. Further, we found that Congress lacked visibility into DOD's process, because there was no requirement for DOD to provide its Biennial Core Report to Congress. We recommended that the Under Secretary of Defense for Acquisition, Technology and Logistics take several actions related to improving the Biennial Core Report, including requiring DOD to compile and report the services' core capability requirements, planned workloads, and any

---

[3]While the statute does not define workload, in this context, DOD defines workload as an amount of depot maintenance work related to specific weapon systems, equipment, components, or programs and to specific services, facilities, and commodities. DOD Instruction 4151.20, *Depot Maintenance Core Capabilities Determination Process* (Jan. 5, 2007).

[4]In this report, we refer to what DOD calls "sustaining workload" as "planned workload to support core capabilities."

[5]GAO, *Depot Maintenance: Actions Needed to Identify and Establish Core Capability at Military Depots*, GAO-09-83 (Washington, D.C.: May 14, 2009).

shortfalls in workloads by work breakdown structure category.[6] We also included a matter for congressional consideration to require DOD to provide this report to Congress. Appendix II provides more information on our recommendations and actions DOD has taken to implement them.

The National Defense Authorization Act for Fiscal Year 2012[7] amended Section 2464 to require DOD to, among other things, submit to Congress a biennial report, no later than April 1 of each even-numbered year. The statute states that DOD is required to identify the following three items for each military service, for the subsequent fiscal year:

1. The core depot-level maintenance and repair capability requirements and sustaining workloads, organized by work breakdown structure expressed in direct labor hours.[8]

2. The corresponding workloads necessary to sustain core depot-level maintenance and repair capability requirements, expressed in direct labor hours and cost.

3. In any case where core depot-level maintenance and repair capability requirements exceed or are expected to exceed sustaining workloads, a detailed rationale for the shortfall and a plan either to correct or mitigate the effects of the shortfall.

In this report, we summarized these three elements as: (1) the required workload to sustain core maintenance capability; (2) the planned workload available; and (3) in any case where the required workload exceeds the planned workload—where there is a shortfall—a detailed explanation of why planned workload is insufficient and a plan to fix the effects of the shortfall.

The statute mandates us to analyze DOD's Biennial Core Report for compliance with the three elements above. In addition, the statute requires us to assess the completeness of the report. The statute further

---

[6]While the statute does not define "work breakdown structure," these structures are groups of categories of equipment and technologies. The categories can be broken down into lower-level elements (levels of indenture) of this equipment and technologies.

[7]Pub. L. No.112-81, § 327 (2011).

[8]While the statute does not define direct labor hours, in this context, DOD defines a direct labor hour as one hour of effort directly attributed to a category of work. DODI 4151.20, *Depot Maintenance Core Capabilities Determination Process* (Jan. 5, 2007).

requires us to provide findings and recommendations after DOD submits its report to Congress. DOD submitted its first Biennial Core Report to Congress on September 4, 2012, and we also received the report on that date.

In response to the mandate, we reviewed the extent to which the report complies with the statutory requirements and is complete. To assess the extent to which DOD's 2012 Biennial Core Report complies with Section 2464, we analyzed the text of the report and obtained information on the process by which DOD identified its essential core capability requirements and the workloads needed to support this core maintenance capability for fiscal year 2013. In those cases where we had determined that the report did not include a required element, we discussed our preliminary analyses with the Office of the Secretary of Defense (OSD) and military service officials to seek additional information. To assess the report's level of completeness, we obtained and analyzed the data and other information that OSD required the military service headquarters to submit in support of the report.

We conducted this performance audit from August 2012 to February 2013 in accordance with generally accepted government auditing standards. Those standards require that we plan and perform the audit to obtain sufficient, appropriate evidence to provide a reasonable basis for our findings and conclusions based on our audit objectives. We believe that the evidence obtained provides a reasonable basis for our findings and conclusions based on our audit objectives. We discuss our scope and methodology in more detail in appendix I.

Background

Determining Core Maintenance Capability

DOD Instruction 4151.20[9] prescribes a "depot maintenance core capabilities determination process" to identify, in part, the (1) required core capabilities for depot maintenance and (2) planned workloads needed to support those capabilities. The instruction describes a series of mathematical computations and adjustments, which the military services

---

[9]DODI 4151.20, *Depot Maintenance Core Capabilities Determination Process* (Jan. 5, 2007).

use to compute their core capability requirements and to identify planned workloads needed to support these requirements. First, the services identify the weapon systems required to execute the Joint Chiefs of Staff contingency[10] scenarios, which represent plans for responding to conflicts that may occur in the future. After the systems are identified, the services compute annual depot maintenance capability requirements for peacetime in direct labor hours to represent the amount of time they regularly take to perform required maintenance. Then contingency requirements and resource[11] adjustments are made to account for applicable surge factors during the different phases of a contingency, such as preparation/readiness and sustainment. Further adjustments are made to account for redundancy in depot capability. For example, a service may determine that repair capabilities for specific systems maintained in military depots are so similar that the capabilities for one system can effectively satisfy the requirements of another. Core capability requirements are also adjusted when one service's maintenance requirements will be supported by the maintenance capabilities of other services.

During this process of identifying the systems for which they will be required to maintain repair capabilities, the services organize and aggregate their capability data by categories of equipment and technologies known as work breakdown structure categories. The work breakdown structure provides a way for DOD to break down a category of weapon system or equipment into subcategories of its parts at increasingly lower levels of detail. The work breakdown structure can be expressed at any level of detail down to the lowest-level part, such as a bolt. These categories, the programs or systems they include, and the lower-level elements or subcategories of defense materiel or equipment into which they are broken down are referred to by DOD as "levels of indenture." There are eleven categories at the top level—"first" level—of the work breakdown structure. A first-level category summarizes information for an entire type of system or equipment, such as aircraft or

---

[10]A contingency is a situation requiring military operations in response to natural disasters, terrorists, subversives, or as otherwise directed by appropriate authority to protect U.S. interests.

[11]A resource, in this context, refers to the personnel, materiel, and other assets or capabilities available to provide depot maintenance.

ground vehicles. Table 1 shows the eleven first-level categories of the work breakdown structure.

Table 1: First-Level Categories of the Work Breakdown Structure

Category number	Work breakdown structure category at the first level
1	Aircraft
2	Ground Vehicles
3	Sea Ships
4	Communication/Electronic Equipment
5	Support Equipment
6	Ordnance, Weapons, & Missiles
7	Software
8	Fabrication/Manufacturing
9	Fleet/Field Support
10	Special Interest Items
11	Other[a]

Source: DOD.

[a]The "Other" category encompasses a number of other items that do not clearly fall under the remaining 10 categories, such as fire trucks, tractors, or missile transport trailers.

A first-level category can be broken down into second-level subcategories, which are the major elements that make up the system or equipment in the first-level category. For example, the first-level category for Aircraft can be broken down into the second-level subcategories for Airframes, Aircraft Components, and Aircraft Engines, which are major elements that make up an aircraft. The second-level subcategories can be further broken down into third-level subcategories, which are subordinate elements that make up the major elements in the second-level categories. For example, the second-level subcategory for Airframes is further divided into the third-level subcategories—different types of airframes, such as Rotary, Fighter/Attack, or Bomber. The subcategories can be further broken down to the lowest-level element of the system. Table 2 shows an example of the top three levels of the work breakdown structure for Aircraft.

Table 2: Example of Category Levels for Aircraft

Level	Category number	Work breakdown structure category
First	1	Aircraft
Second	1.1	Airframes
Third	1.1.1	Rotary
Third	1.1.2	Vertical and/or Short Take-off Landing Aircraft
Third	1.1.3	Cargo/Tanker
Third	1.1.4	Fighter/Attack
Third	1.1.5	Bomber
Third	1.1.6	Aircraft–Other

Source: DOD.

After the services have identified their core capability requirements, they identify the amount of available planned workload within the work breakdown structure categories and subcategories.

Reporting Core Maintenance Capability

DOD Instruction 4151.20 requires the military services to report biennially to OSD their core capability requirements and planned workloads, in accordance with a tasking memorandum issued for each reporting cycle. The instruction includes a worksheet that the services must fill out and submit to OSD. The worksheet calls for information to be organized by the work breakdown structure to various subcategory levels, mostly at the second-level subcategories. Appendix III provides a table listing these categories and subcategories

On April 9, 2012, OSD issued the tasking memorandum for the 2012 Biennial Core Report, which directed the services to use DOD Instruction 4151.20 as basic guidance and included further guidance on how to meet the requirement under Section 2464 to report this information to Congress. The memorandum augments the worksheet by adding another column for the estimated costs of performing the planned workloads at the first level of categories. The instruction and tasking memorandum also require the services to provide additional information when reporting shortfalls in planned workloads. If a military depot does not have sufficient workload to sustain the required level of capability that has been identified, a shortfall exists—in other words, the military depots have not been assigned the depot maintenance workloads that would enable them to sustain their identified core capability requirements. For example, a depot may have identified 10,000 direct labor hours of core capability requirements for ground vehicles but have only 4,000 hours of assigned depot maintenance work for ground vehicles. This depot will have a shortfall of 6,000 hours. The instruction requires that the services report on shortfalls by providing a description along with the worksheet, but the shortfalls are not calculated in the worksheet.

DOD's 2012 Biennial Core Report Partially Complies with Section 2464 and Includes Information for Each of the Military Services

DOD's 2012 Biennial Core Report to Congress complies with two of the required reporting elements of Section 2464—including core capability requirements and planned workload—and partially complies with the third element by including mitigation plans, but not all detailed rationales for workload shortfalls. Further, the report provides complete information for each of the military services as aggregated to the top-level categories of the work breakdown structure. However, without providing clear explanations for the workload shortfalls that clarify why the services do not have the workload to meet core maintenance requirements, DOD's report does not fully comply with Section 2464 and Congress lacks full visibility over DOD's management of its shortfalls.

The Report Includes Information on Core Capability Requirements

OSD included in the report the requirements information expressed in direct labor hours for each of the military services. As reported, DOD's total core capability requirements are about 70 million direct labor hours. Table 3 shows a summary of these core capability requirements by military service.

Table 3: Summary of the Core Report's Core Capability Requirements by Military Service

Military service	Core capability requirements (Direct labor hours)
Army	16,663,845
Navy	30,455,340
Marine Corps	3,337,264
Air Force	19,021,493
Total DOD	**69,477,942**

Source: DOD.

Further, the information in DOD's report on core capability requirements for each of the military services is complete as aggregated to the top-level categories of the work breakdown structure. Section 2464 requires the information in the Biennial Core Report to be organized by work breakdown structure; however, the statute does not specify at which category level of the work breakdown structure the information should be reported. To obtain the information needed to support the 2012 report, OSD's memorandum directed the services to provide to OSD, among other things, information on core requirements and planned workloads at various lower-level subcategories. The memorandum also directed the services to provide, in any instance where core requirements exceed planned workloads, additional information on a plan to address workload shortfalls. Each of the services provided information in response to OSD's memorandum.

The Report Includes Information on the Planned Workloads That Are Available for Supporting Core Capability

In response to the tasking memorandum, the services provided data on their planned workloads—the amount of available work used to maintain the required capability—by the top categories and various levels of subcategories in the work breakdown structure. In the report, OSD included complete information on the amount of planned workload that is available to maintain the required capability, expressed in direct labor hours at the top-level categories and the estimated cost of these workloads for each of the military services. As reported, DOD has a total planned workload of about 92 million direct labor hours at an estimated cost of about $12 billion. Table 4 shows a summary of these workloads.

Table 4: Summary of the Core Report's Planned Workload by Military Service

Military service	Planned workload (direct labor hours)	Estimated cost of planned workload (dollars)
Army	18,464,871	$2,476,607,078
Navy	43,807,318	3,912,871,191
Marine Corps	5,526,905	501,062,333
Air Force	24,588,694	4,758,071,501
Total DOD	92,387,788	$11,649,512,103

Source DOD.

However, we identified an anomaly in the information reported for the Marine Corps. Its planned workload for the sea ships category was reported as 15,124 direct labor hours, without any reported cost. Because the estimated cost of this workload is reported as $0, it is unclear whether the cost for this work is accounted for in DOD's report. OSD and Marine Corps officials stated that the workload hours to do these repairs are to be performed by the Marine Corps for the Navy. The Navy would reimburse the Marine Corps for the workload hours. However, the Navy's submission for the report did not include these workload hours to be performed by the Marine Corps. Thus, these hours and cost were not clearly accounted for in the workload cost figures included in the report. OSD officials stated that they noticed the anomaly, but that their reporting time constraints precluded them from thoroughly investigating it. The report shows that the Navy had a workload of 8.9 million direct labor hours above the core maintenance requirement in the Sea Ships category. Because of this, OSD officials believed that the estimated workload was sufficiently covered and this error would not result in a shortfall.

The Report Includes Information on Shortfalls and Mitigation Plans but Does Not Include Detailed Explanations for Some Shortfalls

While DOD's overall planned workloads exceed its core capability requirements, DOD's report shows shortfalls in certain categories for the Army and the Air Force. The report includes complete information on shortfalls at the top-level categories and plans to mitigate all of the shortfalls identified in the report. However, the report does not include required information on the rationale for some of these shortfalls—the reasons why the services do not have the workloads to meet core maintenance requirements. Section 2464 requires that DOD include in its report "in any case where core depot-level maintenance and repair capability requirements exceed or are expected to exceed sustaining workloads,"—that is, in any case where there are shortfalls—"a detailed rationale for the shortfall and a plan either to correct, or mitigate, the effects of the shortfall."

DOD Reported Workload Shortfalls at Top-Level Categories of the Work Breakdown Structure

Consistent with how it reported the core requirements and planned workloads, OSD aggregated the workload shortfalls under the top-level categories of the work breakdown structure for each service. The report shows that the Navy and Marine Corps did not identify any shortfalls in the workloads available to support their core capability requirements. In assessing the completeness of DOD's report, we determined that the Navy and Marine Corps did not have workload shortfalls at any of the lower-level categories at which they provided information to OSD. The report shows workload shortfalls for the Army and Air Force totaling about 1.4 million direct labor hours. Table 5 shows the shortfalls identified in the report.

Table 5: Summary of the Core Report's Shortfalls by Military Service and Work Breakdown Structure

Direct labor hours

Military service	Work breakdown structure category	Core capability requirement	Planned workload	Workload shortfall
Army	Ground Vehicles	5,704,613	4,835,066	(869,547)
	Support Equipment	1,141,411	1,028,949	(112,462)
Air Force	Communication/ Electronic Equipment	430,330	169,632	(260,698)
	Ordnance, Weapons, & Missiles	958,862	815,582	(143,280)
Total				(1,385,987)

Source: DOD.

In assessing the completeness of DOD's report, we determined that the Army and Air Force identified shortfalls at lower-level subcategories and submitted supplemental information to OSD describing these anticipated shortfalls. For the report, OSD aggregated the information on core requirements and planned workloads provided by the services at the top-level categories of the work breakdown structure. OSD officials told us that the shortfalls included in the report were calculated by taking the difference between the total requirements and planned workload at the top-level categories.

Because of this calculation, some of the workload shortfalls identified by the services at the lower-level categories were balanced out by surplus workload in other lower-level categories under the same top-level category. Thus, these lower-level shortfalls were not included in the report. For the Army, the report showed that there are workload shortfalls of approximately 1 million direct labor hours in the top-level categories for Ground Vehicles and Support Equipment. The Army also submitted information to OSD on additional shortfalls in lower-level subcategories totaling approximately 1.5 million direct labor hours. These shortfalls are anticipated in various third-level subcategories under the top categories of Aircraft; Ground Vehicles; Communication/Electronic Equipment; Support Equipment; and Ordnance, Weapons, and Missiles. For example, the Army identified a shortfall of about 625,000 direct labor hours under the third-level subcategory of Communication Systems Equipment, which is under the top-level category for Communication/Electronics Equipment. For the Air Force, the report reflects total workload shortfalls of approximately 404,000 direct labors hours in the two top-level categories of Communication/Electronic Equipment, and Ordnance, Weapons, and Missiles. However, the Air Force also provided information to OSD on additional shortfalls of about 64,000 direct labor hours for the second-level subcategory of Aircraft Components, under the broader Aircraft category.

OSD officials told us that they chose to report at the top level because they believe this best reflects the services' ability to provide core maintenance, as surplus planned workload in lower-level categories could make up for shortfalls in other categories. They noted that skills, facilities, and equipment are transferrable from one system to another within the top-level category of a work breakdown structure, and that aggregation of workload to the top level presents a more-accurate picture of shortfalls.

The Report Does Not Include Explanations for All Army Shortfalls

The report provides mitigation plans for identified shortfalls in the Army workload but does not provide explanations for all shortfalls to clarify the reasons why the Army does not have sufficient workload to meet core maintenance requirements. The report identifies Army shortfalls of 869,547 direct labor hours that are needed to support its required core maintenance capability to maintain equipment under its Ground Vehicles category of work and 112,462 direct labor hours under its Support Equipment category of work.

Ground Vehicles

The report stated that the shortfall in the Ground Vehicles category includes workload shortfalls for two subcategories—combat vehicles and tactical wheeled vehicles. The report provides both an explanation and a mitigation plan for the shortfall in the combat vehicles subcategory, but does not provide an explanation for the workload shortfalls in the tactical vehicle subcategory. For the combat vehicles shortfall, the report states that the workload shortfall is a result of low usage of ground combat vehicles in current operations. In addition, the report states that in recent years, the Army has executed robust programs to recapitalize and upgrade depot maintenance. Army officials responsible for compiling the Army's input stated that this resulted in positive health and condition of these systems. Because of this low usage and the recent improvements in the systems, the Army anticipates minimal depot repair for these vehicles at this time. The Army plans to mitigate this shortfall by allowing military depot workers to repair similar vehicles that are used to support other maintenance programs.

For tactical wheeled vehicles, the report states that there is a workload shortfall for tactical wheeled vehicles at Red River Army Depot, but does not provide a reason for the shortfall. Army officials stated that the reasons for these shortfalls are the same as the reasons for shortfalls for ground combat vehicles—low usage and recent improvements resulted in reduced workloads in this area. Army officials told us that the Army is anticipating force structure reductions that will significantly lower the amount of tactical wheeled vehicles and result in a lower core maintenance requirement. Army officials told us that the Army is also forming an Integrated Process Team to review the core maintenance requirements for all ground vehicle systems. However, this shortfall mitigation information was not included in the report.

Support Equipment

The report does not clearly provide an explanation for why there is a workload shortfall in the Ground Support Equipment work—why the Army estimates it will not have the workload to meet its core maintenance requirements. The report only states that the shortfall is related to the repairs of the Rhino Passive Infrared Defeat System[12] and Floating Bridges,[13] as well as other repairs for equipment, such as equipment related to bulk petroleum oil and lubricant distribution. Army officials stated that the reasons for these shortfalls are the same as the reasons for the shortfalls for ground vehicles—low usage and recent improvements resulted in reduced workloads in this area. The Army assessed this category to be at minimal risk, and it plans to use similar workloads to mitigate this shortfall. Further, Army officials stated that they project a decrease in core maintenance requirements in this area because of anticipated force structure changes. However, this shortfall mitigation information was not included in DOD's report.

The Report Does Not Include Explanations for All Air Force Shortfalls

The report provides mitigation plans for identified shortfalls in the Air Force core capabilities but does not provide explanations for all of the shortfalls. The report identifies an Air Force shortfall of 260,698 direct labor hours that are needed to support its required core capability for maintaining equipment under its Communication/Electronic Equipment category of work. The report also identifies an additional Air Force workload shortfall of 143,280 direct labor hours that are needed to

---

[12]The Rhino Passive Infrared Defeat System is a capability used to defeat a subset of improvised explosive devices and features a universal bracket that can be mounted on any vehicle platform.

[13]Floating Bridges are structures used for troops, combat materiel, and transport to cross obstacles (such as water barriers, ravines, and roads) while traveling along roads or routes on the field of battle.

support the Air Force's required core capability in maintaining equipment under its Ordnance, Weapons, and Missiles category of work.

Communication/Electronic Equipment

The report does not clearly provide an explanation for why the Air Force anticipates insufficient workload to meet its core maintenance requirements in the Communication/Electronic Equipment category. The report identifies only that the shortfall in communications workload is primarily for unmanned aerial systems ground stations. We asked Air Force officials to clarify the reason for the shortfall, and they told us that the shortfall is caused by the lack of organic (military) depot capability to repair unmanned aerial vehicle ground stations for the anticipated increase in manufacturing of the MQ-1 Predator[14] and MQ-9 Reaper[15] aircraft. According to Air Force officials, contractors currently repair the stations. However, this shortfall explanation information was not included in the report.

The report stated that the Air Force would mitigate the shortfall through incrementally assigning maintenance work to organic (military) depots for the MQ-1 and MQ-9 between the third quarters of fiscal year 2012 through fiscal year 2016. Because the Air Force does not currently have the facilities and personnel at the military depots to execute the identified planned workload, the Air Force also identified a capability shortfall. Air Force officials told us that the Air Force had no scheduled capital investments[16] for the assigned work at the military depots at the time of the report.

---

[14]The MQ-1 Predator is an unmanned aircraft system employed primarily in a killer/scout role as an intelligence collection asset. Each system consists of four sensor/weapon-equipped aircraft, a ground control station, a Predator Primary Satellite Link, and spare equipment.

[15]The MQ-9 Reaper is an unmanned aircraft system designed to provide a ground-attack capability to find, fix, track, target, engage, and assess small ground mobile or fixed targets. Each system consists of four aircraft, a ground control station, and a satellite communications suite.

[16]Capital investment refers to improvements made to facilities or equipment that would make production more efficient or meet expected future needs.

Ordnance, Weapons, and Missiles

The report does not clearly provide an explanation for why the Air Force anticipates insufficient workload to meet its core maintenance requirements in the Ordnance, Weapons, and Missiles category. The report states only that for the Ordnance, Weapons, and Missiles category, the workload shortfall is in missile components. When asked to provide a reason for the shortfall, Air Force officials told us that this shortfall is driven by the lack of organic (military) depot capability for Missile Components work. However, this information is not included in the report.

The Air Force plans to mitigate this shortfall by assigning work to Air Force depots to support existing and new weapon systems, such as missile launchers and defensive missile systems for the MQ-1 Predator and MQ-9 Reaper unmanned aerial systems. According to the report, the Air Force plans to begin the work on the MQ-1 and MQ-9 to mitigate the shortfall in the fourth quarter of fiscal year 2012 and complete this work by fiscal year 2017. Additional work on other aircraft weapon systems, such as for the F-35, will also be used to mitigate this shortfall. This additional work will begin in the first quarter of fiscal year 2013, with full implementation over the following 12-24 months.

In addition, because the Air Force does not currently have the facilities and personnel at the military depots to execute the identified planned workload, it also identified a capability shortfall. Air Force officials told us that the Air Force had no scheduled capital investments for the assigned work at the military depots at the time of the report.

The report does not always include detailed explanations for identified workload shortfalls, because the Army and Air Force did not always provide explanations for them. Without clear explanations for why the services do not have the workload to meet core maintenance requirements, Congress does not have visibility whether the services' plans to correct or mitigate the shortfalls will address the cause of the shortfalls.

Conclusions

Section 2464, among other things, requires DOD to maintain a core maintenance capability that is government-owned and government-operated, assign sufficient workload to support this capability, and report information on this capability to Congress. DOD's first report to Congress includes most of the required elements. However, it did not provide explanations for all of the identified workload shortfalls. Clear reasons for why the services do not have the workload to meet core maintenance requirements would provide key information for Congress about how the services' plans to correct or mitigate the shortfalls would be addressing the cause of the shortfalls. Without complete and clear information on this element of the statute, Congress may lack full visibility into the status of DOD's management of its core capabilities.

Recommendation for Executive Action

To ensure that Congress has visibility over the status of DOD's core depot-level maintenance and repair capability, we recommend that the Secretary of Defense direct the Deputy Assistant Secretary of Defense (Maintenance, Policy, and Programs) to include in the Biennial Core Report to Congress detailed explanations for why services do not have the workload to meet core maintenance requirements for each shortfall identified in the report.

Agency Comments

We provided a draft of this report to DOD for comment. In its written comments, reproduced in appendix IV, DOD concurred with our recommendation and stated that the department will include an explanation and mitigation plan for each workload shortfall identified in all future reports.

We are sending copies of this report to the appropriate congressional committees; the Secretary of Defense; the Deputy Assistant Secretary of Defense (Maintenance, Policy, and Programs); the Secretaries of the Army, Navy, and Air Force and the Commandant of the Marine Corps; and other interested parties. In addition, the report is available at no charge on the GAO website at http://www.gao.gov.

If you or your staff have any questions about this report, please contact me at (202) 512-5257 or merrittz@gao.gov. Contact points for our Offices of Congressional Relations and Public Affairs may be found on the last page of this report. GAO staff who made key contributions to this report are listed in appendix V.

Zina D. Merritt
Director
Defense Capabilities and Management

List of Committees

The Honorable Carl Levin
Chairman
The Honorable James Inhofe
Ranking Member
Committee on Armed Services
United States Senate

The Honorable Chairman
The Honorable Ranking Member
Subcommittee on Defense
Committee on Appropriations
United States Senate

The Honorable Howard P. "Buck" McKeon
Chairman
The Honorable Adam Smith
Ranking Member
Committee on Armed Services
House of Representatives

The Honorable C.W. Bill Young
Chairman
The Honorable Pete Visclosky
Ranking Member
Subcommittee on Defense
Committee on Appropriations
House of Representatives

Appendix I: Scope and Methodology

To determine the extent to which the Department of Defense's (DOD) 2012 Biennial Core Report complies with Section 2464 of Title 10 of the United States Code and includes service data and information required by DOD to support the report, we analyzed the text of DOD's Biennial Core Report and obtained supporting information on DOD's core determination process for 2013. One of our analysts reviewed DOD's report to determine the extent to which it included each element of the mandate, and a second analyst reviewed the first analyst's conclusions. All initial disagreements between analysts were discussed and resolved through consensus. When the report explicitly included all parts of the mandated element, our assessment is that DOD "complied" with the element. When the report did not explicitly include any part of the element, our assessment is that DOD "did not comply" with the element. If the report included some aspects of an element, but not all, then our assessment is that DOD "partially complied" with the element. We checked to see that the services were each providing the same type of information.

To assess the level of completeness of the information, we obtained and analyzed the data and other information that the Office of the Secretary of Defense (OSD) required the military service headquarters to provide in support of the report. We compared the services' submissions to the reporting template in DOD Instruction 4151.20[1] in order to determine the extent to which the services submitted information required by DOD's instruction and identify any inconsistencies or errors. We conducted data-reliability assessments for all the data analyzed and reported upon by performing independent reliability assessments through which individual team members reviewed the services' submissions to determine (1) whether the requirements were met, and (2) the extent to which the data that was provided supports the responses. The team also reviewed the data provided by the services to OSD to support their respective responses for the Biennial Core Report. Individual team members compared the data provided to OSD to the data published in the report to ensure consistency. The team also met with knowledgeable officials to obtain clarification and understanding of the content of the submissions. From these analyses, the team concluded that the data were sufficiently reliable for the purposes of this report.

---

[1]DOD Instruction 4151.20, *Depot Maintenance Core Capabilities Determination Process* (Jan. 5, 2007).

We conducted this performance audit from August 2012 to February 2013 in accordance with generally accepted government auditing standards. Those standards require that we plan and perform the audit to obtain sufficient, appropriate evidence to provide a reasonable basis for our findings and conclusions based on our audit objectives. We believe that the evidence obtained provides a reasonable basis for our findings and conclusions based on our audit objectives.

Appendix II: Prior GAO Work on Core Logistics Capability

In 2009, we reported that the Department of Defense (DOD), through its biennial core process, had not comprehensively and accurately assessed whether it had the required core capability to support fielded systems in military depots.[1] We found that, among other things,

- DOD's method of compiling and internally reporting core requirements and associated workloads did not reveal specific shortfalls; and
- Congress lacked visibility of DOD's core process, because there was no requirement for DOD to provide its Biennial Core Report to Congress.

We recommended that the Under Secretary of Defense for Acquisition, Technology and Logistics take several actions related to improving the Biennial Core Report, including requiring DOD to compile and report the services' core capability requirements, planned workloads, and any shortfalls by work breakdown structure category, and requiring DOD to provide this report to Congress. Table 6 details the three recommendations and one matter for congressional consideration we made in our 2009 report that are relevant to this review of the Biennial Core Report, and the respective actions taken by DOD.

---

[1]GAO, *Depot Maintenance: Actions Needed to Identify and Establish Core Capability at Military Depots*, GAO-09-83 (Washington, D.C.: May 14, 2009).

Table 6: GAO's 2009 Recommendations, Matter for Consideration, and DOD's Actions to Improve DOD's Report on Core Capability Requirements

Recommendations[a]	Actions taken
Require DOD to compile and report the services' core capability requirements, planned organic workloads, and any shortfalls by equipment/technology category (work breakdown structure).	Implemented: Assistant Secretary of Defense for Logistics and Materiel Readiness tasked the services in an April 2012 memorandum to report core capability requirements by work breakdown structure.
Require DOD to implement internal controls to prevent errors and inconsistencies in the services' core calculations. At a minimum, internal controls should address errors and inconsistencies identified in our review relating to the need to include (1) all Joint Chiefs of Staff-scenario-tasked systems, (2) software maintenance requirements, and (3) only public depot maintenance workload when adjusting for redundancy.	Implemented: Assistant Secretary of Defense for Logistics and Materiel Readiness tasked the services in a March 2010 memorandum to include all Joint Staff–tasked systems and software maintenance requirements as part of the core logistics capabilities. Also, the memorandum tasked the services to only consider organic (public) depot maintenance workloads when adjusting for redundant capability.
Explicitly state the mathematical calculations, based on their core determination worksheets, which the services should use to determine core capability requirements, associated workload, and shortfalls, if any.	Implemented: Assistant Secretary of Defense for Logistics and Materiel Readiness tasked the services in a March 2010 memorandum to use the tables from DOD Instruction 4151.20. The services were instructed to fully complete those tables in their entirety in their format and provide their responses in both Excel spreadsheet and hardcopy.
Matter for congressional consideration	**Actions taken**
Congress should consider requiring DOD to report on the status of its effort to maintain a core logistics capability consistent with Section 2464 of Title 10, U.S. Code. In doing so, Congress may wish to require that DOD report biennially on the results of its core determination process, actions taken to correct any identified shortfalls in core capability, and efforts to identify and establish core capability for new and modified systems in a timely manner, consistent with DOD guidance	Implemented: The National Defense Authorization Act for Fiscal Year 2012, Pub. L. No. 112-81, amended Section 2464 of Title 10 of the United States Code to require that the Secretary of Defense submit to Congress a biennial report identifying core depot-level maintenance capabilities and the workloads required to sustain those capabilities. The congressional report is required no later than April 1 on each even-numbered year detailing core capability requirements. In September 2012, the Under Secretary of Defense (Acquisition, Technology & Logistics) issued the first Biennial Core Report to Congress.

Source: GAO.

[a]GAO reported a total of eight recommendations and one matter for congressional consideration. We only included three recommendations and the matter for congressional consideration because they were based on improving the Biennial Core Report.

Appendix III: Category Levels from DOD's 2012 Depot Maintenance Core Capability Worksheet

Work Breakdown Structure Category
1. Aircraft
1.1 Airframes
1.1.1 Rotary
1.1.2 Vertical/Short Take-Off and Landing
1.1.3 Cargo/Tanker
1.1.4 Fighter/Attack
1.1.5 Bomber
1.1.6 Aircraft - Other
1.2 Aircraft Components
1.2.1 Dynamic Components
1.2.2 Hydraulic/Pneumatic
1.2.3 Instruments
1.2.4 Landing Gear
1.2.5 Aviation Ordnance
1.2.6 Avionics/Electronics
1.2.7 Auxiliary Power Units
1.2.8 Other
1.3 Aircraft Engines
2. Ground Vehicles
2.1 Combat Vehicles
2.2 Amphibious Vehicles
2.3 Tactical (wheeled) Vehicles
2.4 Construction Equipment
3. Sea Ships
3.1 Aircraft Carriers
3.2 Submarines
3.3 Surface Combatants/Others
4. Communication/Electronic Equipment
4.1 Radar
4.2 Radio
4.3 Wire
4.4 Electronic Warfare
4.5 Navigational Aids
4.6 Electro-Optics/Night Vision
4.7 Crypto
4.8 Computers

	4.9 Other
5.	Support Equipment
	5.1 Ground Support Equipment
	5.2 Generators
	5.3 Test, Measurement, and Diagnostic Equipment
	5.4 Calibration
	5.5 Other
6.	Ordnance, Weapons, & Missiles
	6.1 Nuclear Weapons
	6.2 Chemical Weapons
	6.3 Biological Weapons
	6.4 Conventional Weapons
	6.5 Explosives
	6.6 Small Arms/Personal Weapons
	6.7 Strategic Missiles
	6.8 Tactical Missiles
7.	Software
	7.1 Weapon System
	7.2 Support Equipment
8.	Fabrication/Manufacturing
9.	Fleet/Field Support
10.	Special Interest Items
11.	Other

Source: DOD.

Appendix IV: Comments from the Department of Defense

ASSISTANT SECRETARY OF DEFENSE
3500 DEFENSE PENTAGON
WASHINGTON, DC 20301-3500

LOGISTICS AND
MATERIEL READINESS

JAN 2 4 2013

Ms. Zina D. Merrit
Director
Defense Capabilities and Management
U.S. Government Accountability Office
441 G Street, N.W.
Washington, DC 20548

Dear Ms. Merrit:

This is the Department of Defense (DoD) response to the U.S. Government

Accountability Office (GAO) Draft Report, GAO-13-194, "DEPOT MAINTENANCE:

Additional Information Needed to Meet DoD's Core Capability Reporting Requirements," dated

December 21, 2012 (GAO Code 351717). The Department concurs with the GAO

recommendation and appreciates the opportunity to comment on the GAO Draft Report. Official

written comments are enclosed. My point of contact in this matter is Ms. Corey Battistoni,

Maintenance Policy and Programs, at 703-614-9329.

Sincerely,

Alan F. Estevez

Enclosure:
As stated

U.S. GOVERNMENT ACCOUNTABILITY OFFICE (GAO) DRAFT REPORT
DATED DECEMBER 21, 2012
GAO-13-194 (GAO CODE 351717)

"DEPOT MAINTENANCE: ADDITIONAL INFORMATION NEEDED TO
MEET DOD'S CORE CAPABILITY REPORTING REQUIREMENTS"

DEPARTMENT OF DEFENSE COMMENTS
TO THE GAO RECOMMENDATIONS

RECOMMENDATION: The GAO recommends that the Secretary of Defense direct
the Deputy Assistant Secretary of Defense (Maintenance, Policy, and Programs) to
include in the Biennial Core Report to Congress detailed explanations for why services
do not have the workload to meet core maintenance requirements for each shortfall
identified in the report.

DoD RESPONSE: Concur. The Department will include an explanation and mitigation
plan for each workload shortfall identified in all future reports.

Appendix V: GAO Contact and Staff Acknowledgments

GAO Contact	Zina D. Merritt, (202) 512-5257 or merrittz@gao.gov
Staff Acknowledgments	In addition to the contact named above, Carleen Bennett, Assistant Director; Gina Hoffman; Joanne Landesman; Jennifer Madison; Michael Silver; Jose Watkins; and Michael Willems made key contributions to this report.

Related GAO Products

Defense Logistics: DOD Input Needed on Implementing Depot Maintenance Study Recommendations. GAO-11-568R. Washington, D.C.: June 30, 2011.

Depot Maintenance: Actions Needed to Identify and Establish Core Capability at Military Depots. GAO-09-83. Washington, D.C.: May 14, 2009.

DOD Civilian Personnel: Improved Strategic Planning Needed to Help Ensure Viability of DOD's Civilian Industrial Workforce. GAO-03-472. Washington, D.C.: April 30, 2003.

GAO's Mission	The Government Accountability Office, the audit, evaluation, and investigative arm of Congress, exists to support Congress in meeting its constitutional responsibilities and to help improve the performance and accountability of the federal government for the American people. GAO examines the use of public funds; evaluates federal programs and policies; and provides analyses, recommendations, and other assistance to help Congress make informed oversight, policy, and funding decisions. GAO's commitment to good government is reflected in its core values of accountability, integrity, and reliability.
Obtaining Copies of GAO Reports and Testimony	The fastest and easiest way to obtain copies of GAO documents at no cost is through GAO's website (http://www.gao.gov). Each weekday afternoon, GAO posts on its website newly released reports, testimony, and correspondence. To have GAO e-mail you a list of newly posted products, go to http://www.gao.gov and select "E-mail Updates."
Order by Phone	The price of each GAO publication reflects GAO's actual cost of production and distribution and depends on the number of pages in the publication and whether the publication is printed in color or black and white. Pricing and ordering information is posted on GAO's website, http://www.gao.gov/ordering.htm.
	Place orders by calling (202) 512-6000, toll free (866) 801-7077, or TDD (202) 512-2537.
	Orders may be paid for using American Express, Discover Card, MasterCard, Visa, check, or money order. Call for additional information.
Connect with GAO	Connect with GAO on Facebook, Flickr, Twitter, and YouTube. Subscribe to our RSS Feeds or E-mail Updates. Listen to our Podcasts. Visit GAO on the web at www.gao.gov.
To Report Fraud, Waste, and Abuse in Federal Programs	Contact: Website: http://www.gao.gov/fraudnet/fraudnet.htm E-mail: fraudnet@gao.gov Automated answering system: (800) 424-5454 or (202) 512-7470
Congressional Relations	Katherine Siggerud, Managing Director, siggerudk@gao.gov, (202) 512-4400, U.S. Government Accountability Office, 441 G Street NW, Room 7125, Washington, DC 20548
Public Affairs	Chuck Young, Managing Director, youngc1@gao.gov, (202) 512-4800 U.S. Government Accountability Office, 441 G Street NW, Room 7149 Washington, DC 20548

Please Print on Recycled Paper.